MUTED VOICE

STUDY GUIDE

A Challenge to the Body of Christ

to Speak Out Against Racism

Mike Moore

MIKE MOORE
MINISTRIES

Muted Voice Study Guide

Copyright © 2020 by Mike Moore

Published in the United States by Mike Moore Ministries, Inc.
www.mikemooreministries.org

ISBN 978-1-7333716-3-6

Any internet addresses (websites, blogs, etc.) in this book are offered as a resource. They are not intended in any way to be or imply an endorsement by Mike Moore Ministries, nor does Mike Moore Ministries vouch for the content of these sites for the life of this book.

Unless otherwise indicated, all Scripture quotations are taken from the New King James Version, © 1979, 1980, 1982, 1984 by Thomas Nelson, Inc. Used by permission. All rights reserved.
Scriptures marked KJV are taken from the KING JAMES VERSION (KJV): KING JAMES VERSION, public domain.

Scriptures marked (NKJV) are taken from the New King James Version®. Copyright © 1982 by Thomas Nelson. Used by permission. All rights reserved.

Scriptures marked (NLT) are taken from the Holy Bible, New Living Translation, copyright © 1996, 2004, 2007, 2013, 2015 by Tyndale House Foundation. Used by permission of Tyndale House Publishers Inc., Carol Stream, Illinois 60188. All rights reserved.

Scriptures marked CEV are taken from the CONTEMPORARY ENGLISH VERSION (CEV): Scripture taken from the CONTEMPORARY ENGLISH VERSION copyright© 1995 by the American Bible Society. Used by permission.

Scripture taken from The Message (MSG). Copyright Â© 1993, 1994, 1995, 1996, 2000, 2001, 2002. Used by permission of NavPress Publishing Group.

Printed in the United States of America

MUTED V⊛ICE

TABLE OF CONTENTS

INTRODUCTION

I feel called by God to challenge the Body of Christ to speak out against racism. He said to me, **"a muted voice is no voice."** When we look at the Body of Christ and the Church's response to racial inequality and injustice, we see and hear silence. **YOU** are the Body of Christ. My prayer is for this study guide to be a tool to…

- Help you gain knowledge about racism
- Cause introspection through self-reflection
- Stimulate learning through thought-provoking questions
- Assist you in mind renewal and growth
- Provide you with practical examples
- Encourage you to take actions

*And do not be conformed to this world, but be transformed by the **renewing** of your **mind**, that you may prove what is that good and acceptable and perfect will of God. (Romans 12:2 NKJV)*

NOTE: All people of color experience racism. However, in this guide, we are specifically addressing racism between Black and White people since those two groups show a stark difference in how they view race relations.

HOW TO USE THIS GUIDE

To get the best results from this guide, be sure to **be honest with yourself** when answering the questions. This is the only way growth will occur. You can either answer the questions inside of this guide or use your laptop/notepad, the choice is yours.

Be on the lookout for the SELF-REFLECTION and the ONE ACTION sections at the end of each of the seven sessions. These sections are intended to help you to maximize the impact.
To enrich your experience, you may use this guide along with the FREE *Muted Voice Docuseries* at **www.mutedvoice.info**.

Let's get started!

SESSION 1 – WHAT IS RACISM?

America is in a national crisis. Following the murder of George Floyd on May 25, 2020, mass protests in the United States turned into a global movement for racial equality. An unusual awareness of racial injustice has created a desire for reformation across large spectrums of society including government, education, the military, business arenas, sports, and entertainment.

Many institutions in our present day are speaking out against racism. Businesses are changing the names of racially offensive products, advertisements, etc. But when you look at the Church's response, we see and hear silence.

A MUTED VOICE

Imagine yourself sitting in your recliner watching your favorite show or movie and you mistakenly hit the mute button. Although you can still see what is happening on the screen, you are unable to hear the sound or voices. When it comes to racism, the Church has a muted voice.

Q: What is a **MUTED** voice?

A: A MUTED voice is NO voice. A MUTED voice is a silent voice that refrains from speech and refrains from utterance.

POWER POINT:

A silent voice is left open to interpretation. The Church's silence on the matter of racism can be viewed as complicit, insensitive, and passive.

Do you think the Church's muted voice is an accurate response to racism? Why or why not?

_____

_____

Do you think the Church should be the greatest influencer to bring racial equality? Why or why not?

_____

_____

RACISM

It is important to educate yourself when it comes to racism. What is racism? If you took a poll of five people, you would probably get five different answers. Everyone has assumptions, attitudes, and beliefs about it. But are your assumptions and beliefs accurate?

Racism can occur at both an unconscious and conscious level. It is possible to be racist and not know it. Therefore, an accurate understanding of racism is critical.

Before we go further, how would you define racism? What does it mean to you?

_____

_____

_____

Racism can be defined as:

- The belief that race and skin color accounts for differences in human character, intelligence, ability, beauty, or civility that results in partiality toward one race and prejudice against another.
- "A power relationship or struggle between groups of people who are competing for resources and political power." - Dr. Claud Anderson
- Attributing different (positive or negative) qualities to different racial groups.
- The belief that one race is innately superior to another race.

Take a moment to compare the definitions. Are there any contradictions in your assumptions? Are there any adjustments you need to make in your thinking or actions? If so, what are they?

_____

_____

_____

THE OFFSPRING OF RACISM

For a further understanding of what racism means, we will discuss the offspring of racism which includes **prejudice**, **hatred**, and **discrimination**.

- **Prejudice has to do with "THOUGHTS."** It is prejudgment or preconceived negative opinions about someone not based in facts, or personal knowledge or experience, but based on hearsay, stereotypes, and generalizations.

  Example: Have you ever heard someone say Asians are very smart, Black people are extremely athletic, White people cannot dance, or Jewish people are stingy?

- **Hatred has to do with "FEELINGS."** It is deep, negative emotions or hostilities felt toward particular races of people. *(Ex. white supremacist groups);* or mild discomfort or uneasiness around certain groups of people that prompt you to segregate or withdraw from them
  Example: "White Flight" - when White people move from a neighborhood once the area becomes racially diverse.

  Hatred can be expressed with deep negative emotions OR with **subtlety**. The voice of hatred sounds like: "*I don't like being around those people,*" or "*I believe you should just stay with your own kind.*"

- **Discrimination has to do with "ACTIONS."** It is natural responses based on prejudice. *Example: Ignoring, exclusion, withdrawing, threats, ridicule, slander, violence* **Example:** *Country clubs not accepting someone's membership application because of the person's race.*

When you hear the words prejudice, hatred, and discrimination, what thoughts come to your mind?

_____

_____

_____

Based on the definitions of the offspring of racism, have you ever consciously or unconsciously engaged in racism? How do you feel about that?

_____

_____

_____

Have you ever experienced acts of racism?

_____

Have you witnessed acts of racism? If so, what was your response? Did you prevent it? Did you name it as racism while it was happening? Why or why not?

_____

_____

_____

Why don't people stop acts of racism?

_____

_____

_____

Was the murder of George Floyd an act of racism? Explain your answer.

_____

_____

_____

RACISM = ANTI-EQUALITY

POWER POINT:

God reveals His character, thoughts, and perspective through His Word. Racism is against the biblical position of **equality in-Christ.**

The Bible is God's Word to us. As Christians, we are not to decide how we live. Our thoughts and actions should align with His Word. **The following Scriptures reveal there is complete equality in the Body of Christ.**

- "And He has made from one blood, every nation of men to dwell on all the face of the earth…" Acts 17:26 NKJV
- "In Christ family, there can be no division into Jew and non-Jew, slave and free, male and female. Among us you are **all** equal." Galatians 3:28 (MSG)

IN CLOSING

In response to racism, the Church's voice has been muted. The Church's silence on the matter of racism can be viewed as complicit, insensitive, and passive. Have you been silent? It is racist to be aware of a biased situation and permit it to exist. This is passive racism. It is important for you as a Christian to align your thoughts with God thoughts. His thought is racism equals anti-equality.

11

SELF-REFLECTION

The protests in America in 2020 are related to police brutality against Black people. What are your thoughts and feelings about the protests?

_____

_____

_____

What are your thoughts on the topic of racial inequality in the United States of America and the Church's muted voice?

_____

_____

_____

Be honest. Say your response while looking in the mirror. Are your thoughts and behaviors surrounding race and racial inequities consistent with God's Word? If not, are you willing to make a change? Explain your answer.

_____

_____

_____

How does your response make you feel?
Example: *Happy, comfortable, dissatisfied, sad, motivated*

_____

_____

If someone of a different racial background read your response, how would they feel? If your response is "yes, my thoughts and behavior concerning race and racial inequities are consistent with God's Word," would that person agree with your answer? Are you sure? How do you know?

If your thoughts do not reflect God's thoughts, here are a few suggestions:

- *Watch Episode 1 of the **Muted Voice** docuseries at **www.mutedvoice.info**. It includes an example of a modern-day illustration of racism involving Colin Kaerpernick and an in-depth explanation of the lie that silenced the Church (The Curse of Ham).*
- *Meditate on Acts 17:26, Galatians 3:28 (Message Bible)*
- *Pray*

ONE ACTION

What is one thing that you can do that will help you to step outside of your comfort zone and practice what you have learned from this session? Do one of the examples below or come up with your own.

Examples:

Strike up a conversation with a person of a different race at the store.

Ask a co-worker from a different race to go to lunch. Attend a diverse church.

Invite someone of the opposite race to your church.

Start a small group or ask your Pastor about ways your church can begin or continue discussions on racial injustice.

Ask your employer about ways you can start discussions about racial injustices in the workplace.

SESSION 2 – THE PREVALENCE OF INFECTION

In Session 1, we discovered that in response to racism, the Church's voice has been muted. This silence on the matter of racism can be viewed as complicit, insensitive, and passive. **Silence is a form of racism.**

POWER POINT:

The infection of racism in America has spread across the Church.

Why is the Church's Voice Muted? It is muted due to the infection of racism. Racism has infiltrated and influenced many institutions, including the Christian Church. The prevalence of infection in medical terms, has to do with the percentage of individuals in a population infected with a given pathogen or medical condition. (For instance, COVID-19 infiltrated the entire world.)

The challenge is infection can have devastating economic and social impacts. Can you think of other devastating impacts that a widespread infection could have?

_____

_____

_____

HOW WIDESPREAD IS RACISM IN THE CHURCH?

Think for a moment. How widespread do you think racism is in the Church?

_____

_____

In 1963, Dr. Martin Luther King, Jr. said, "the most segregated hour of Christian America is eleven o'clock on Sunday morning." However, today churches remain overwhelmingly racially divided.

Consider the following stats:

- 90% of African American Christians worship in all Black churches.
- 90% of White American Christians worship in all White churches.

1 CORINTHIANS 1:10 (NKJV)

Now I plead with you, brethren, by the name of our Lord Jesus Christ, that you all speak the same thing, **and *that* there be no divisions among you,** but *that* you be perfectly joined together in the same mind and in the same judgment.

There is a real problem with these statistics. According to 1 Corinthians 1:10, the Black Church and the White Church are a distortion of God's original intent. God's vision for the Church, the Body of Christ, is UNITY and that there be no division named among us.

Think about Dr. Martin Luther King, Jr.'s statement. Decades later, why do you think there is still racial division in the Church?

_____

_____

The Body of Christ is multicolored and multiracial. If you invited Jesus Christ to your church, would it reflect that? What would He see?

_____

_____

POWER POINT:

The greatest sin in the Body of Christ and the greatest threat to God's plan of revival in the United States is racism. Why? In Psalm 133:1, and John 17:21-23, God connects His anointing, productivity, blessings, glory, and the Believers and the churches witness to *oneness and unity.*

In Acts 13:1, the first Christian church in Antioch was a multiracial, multi-ethnic Christian church. Two (2) of the five (5) leaders mentioned in the church of Antioch were Black.

How might you personally be preventing oneness in the Church?

_____

_____

_____

How can you help to build oneness?

_____

_____

_____

HOW DID THE CHURCH GET INFECTED?

There are **four (4) Social Viruses of Racism** that contribute to the infectious spread of racism in the Church.

1. Generational Racism
2. Environmental Racism
3. Institutional Racism
4. Reactionary Racism

GENERATIONAL RACISM

Read Jeremiah 16:19 (KJV). It says, "surely our fathers have inherited lies..."

Generational Racism is when beliefs, attitudes, and false concepts of others are passed from one generation to the next through teaching, modeling, and experience.

In the field of social science, ***generational racism*** is the byproduct, the result of negative racial socialization. Racial and ethnic socialization (RES) involves the direct and explicit messages and indirect and implicit messages children receive about race and certain groups of people in society.

All children are socialized and gain information about racial groups from parents, family members, teachers, clergy, coaches, media, TV, news, advertisements, publications, and more.

Example(s):

- When a child looks at a magazine, and his or her race is highly represented, that is an indirect message.
- When a child looks at a beauty pageant and the representation is low, that is an indirect implicit message.

Describe ways in which children have received implicit messages about race in society.

_____

_____

_____

What direct and indirect messages are being sent to children when White people are represented more than Black people?

_____

_____

_____

17

Share your experiences regarding the representation of White people and underrepresentation of Black people (on TV, in media, in leadership positions, etc.). Describe how those experiences subconsciously shaped your views regarding both White and Black people.

_____

_____

_____

How are people of color portrayed in the media? Is it generally positive or negative? Stereotypes?

_____

_____

What messages do children receive about race from the Church?

_____

_____

_____

Can you recognize ways in which false concepts of racial groups have been passed down in your family? In what ways can you prevent these from being passed down going forward?

_____

_____

_____

As a parent, future parent, family member, teacher, or member of the clergy, how can you ensure you do not perpetuate the cycle of generational racism?

_____

_____

_____

Although we may think in the ways we have been socialized or conditioned to think, we are responsible for changing these attitudes through deeper introspection and acknowledgement of any lingering and sometimes subtle prejudices.

What are your current thoughts about yourself, and others outside of your race? Do you believe any stereotypes or generalizations (positive or negative) about certain racial groups? Write your thoughts down, then think about whether you need to disrupt them or not.

_____

_____

_____

The Body of Christ is multicolored and multiracial. However, our upbringing, family, friends, schools, and churches from which we develop our worldview are often not so diverse. Did your background expose you to the many textures of God's human family? If not, what keeps you in your box?

School

Family

Friends

Church

_____

_____

_____

_____

_____

What are 3 things you can do in the next 30 days to come out of the box (i.e. expose yourself to diversity and disparities)?

Example(s):

- *Read a book about a culture totally different that yours.*

- *Ask someone of a different race and a different worldview about their personal experience concerning race. Listen to them without interruption.*
- *Go to the toy section of a store and see how many dolls represent your race versus another race.*

_____

_____

_____

ENVIRONMENTAL RACISM

Environmental racism occurs when racial beliefs, attitudes, and behaviors are shaped or influenced by one's environment, associations, and words.

HISTORY HUDDLE - RACISM IN THE BIBLE

DID YOU KNOW?

o **In the New Testament, the Jews did not associate with Gentiles. The Jews believed they were the superior race, and Gentiles were the inferior race.**

Acts 11:3 (KJV)
[3] saying, Thou wentest in to men uncircumcised, and didst eat with them.

o No Orthodox Jew would cohabitate, engage, or associate with Gentiles.

o In Acts 10, the Holy Spirit told Peter (a Jew) to go to a Gentile's house and share the Gospel.

o **Peter obeyed and there was a great outpouring of the Spirit, but when he came back to Jerusalem his Jewish brothers reprimanded him for associating with Gentiles (Acts 11:3).**

20

Did you grow up in a home or environment where you heard your parents, siblings, or peers say negative, disparaging words about groups of people by race or ethnicity? If so, what were the words? Did you realize the words were disparaging?

Example(s): *"She is pretty for a Black girl." "You know how **they** are."*

What impact has it had on you personally?

_____

_____

*Have you ever felt pressure to conform to your environment from family members, peers, and/or affiliations? (**Example:** "Stay with your own kind.")*

_____

- *What did you do and why did you do it?*

     _____

     _____

     _____

Can you think of a specific example, from your own experience, church, or community of environmental racism? How did it make you feel?

_____

_____

_____

Removing personal biases, how can Church environments counteract racism?

_____

_____

_____

INSTITUTIONAL RACISM

Institutional racism is racism as a structure (not an event). **Institutional racism** is a racism that is a **SYSTEM** that functions and goes well beyond individuals, group-level structure, and processes that reproduce racial inequalities.

In White Fragility, Robin DiAngelo defines **institutional racism** as, "*collective prejudice backed by legal authority and institutional control.*" Institutional Control involves:

- **Position control** – White people control all of the major institutions in America (business and finance, government, military, media, education, judicial system, medicine, sports, entertainment, etc.)
- **Authority control** - White people set the laws, policies, practices, and norms that others must live by.

Examples of institutional racism are found in educational inequalities, disproportionate Black arrests and convictions, housing disparities, employment and hiring practices, etc.

Institutional racism is a system of *advantage* based on race, and often this advantage is referred to as **"White privilege"** – advantages that are taken for granted by White people but not enjoyed by people of color.

What emotions arise when you hear the term "White privilege?"

_____

_____

_____

Have you witnessed or experienced institutional/systemic racism in your own life? If so, think about it and explain how it did or did not impact you.

_____

_____

_____

Can you think of any current and/or past national or community occurrences that are instances of institutional racism? Explain.

_____

_____

_____

What can be done to bring awareness and solutions in your sphere of influence?

_____

_____

_____

Has institutional/systemic racism helped the spread of racism in the Church? If so, how?

_____

_____

_____

How has the Church helped the spread of racism in society in a systemic way?

_____

_____

_____

REACTIONARY RACISM

Reactionary racism is responding to bias with bias and responding to prejudice with prejudice. It is responding to injustice with violence, retaliation, and generalizations.

Example: "You hate me, and I hate you."

EXODUS 21:24 (KJV)

[24] eye for eye, tooth for tooth, hand for hand, foot for foot

However, according to the Bible, God commands us to LOVE and react in love towards others.

Three (3) points to remember:

- All White people are not racist.
- All Black people are not violent.
- All police officers are not abusive.

A WORD TO BLACK CHRISTIANS

As a Black Christian, you do not have the right to hate anyone, regardless of what is done to you.

- According to the Bible, we must react in love towards **everyone**.

    NOTE: This does not necessarily mean that you should VOTE for a disrespectful politician.

- This also does not mean that you should even respect a disrespectful person.

- NOTE: The Bible never instructs the Believer to respect, disrespect. Love and respect are not the same thing. **You do not have to respect, disrespect.**

GALATIANS 6:7 (KJV)

[7]Be not deceived; God is not mocked: for whatsoever a man soweth, that shall he also reap.

How should Black Christians respond to disrespect?

1. Be angry, but do not sin by reacting with violence, retaliation, and generalizations.

2. Quickly resolve anger by channeling it in a positive way.

3. Do not allow anger to develop into bitterness.
   NOTE: Unresolved anger, bitterness, and hate hinder the Black Christian from moving forward, and they hinder God from working in your life (Hebrews 12:15).

EPHESIANS 4:26 (KJV)

[15]**Be ye angry, and sin not**: let not the sun go down upon your wrath...

HEBREWS 12:15 (KJV)

[15]looking diligently lest any man fail of the grace of God; **lest any root of bitterness springing up trouble you**, and thereby many be defiled.

Recall moments in which you were disrespected by a member of another racial group. Describe your positive or negative reactions.

_____

_____

_____

_____

Have you allowed anger to cause you to react in retaliation or develop into bitterness? If not, explain. If so, have you inappropriately justified it in your mind? Please explain.

_____

_____

_____

Think about and list techniques you can use to resolve anger by channeling it in a positive way.

_____

_____

_____

A WORD TO WHITE CHRISTIANS

As a White Christian, when someone is being racially insensitive, mean, and speaking negatively about people and you applaud and cheer, you are guilty and complicit in that person's meanness.

Whether the person is the president, a leader, politician, pastor, or parent, meanness is meanness. This is extremely harmful. It causes division and it is not the heart of God. You do not have the right to rename meanness and call it **boldness.**

Meditating on the following Scriptures will help Christians to be led by the Word of God (not a person) and properly react to mean racists.

Proverbs 18:21 (KJV)	Death and life are in the power of the tongue: and they that love it shall eat the fruit thereof.
Matthew 12:34-37 (KJV)	[34] O generation of vipers, how can ye, being evil, speak good things? **for out of the abundance of the heart the mouth speaketh.** [35] A good man out of the good treasure of the heart bringeth forth good things: and an evil man out of the evil treasure bringeth forth evil things. [36] But I say unto you, That every idle word that men shall speak, they shall give account thereof in the day of judgment. [37] For by thy words thou shalt be justified, and by thy words thou shalt be condemned.
Ephesians 4:29 (KJV)	**Let no corrupt communication proceed out of your mouth,** but that which is good to the use of edifying, that it may minister grace unto the hearers.
Ephesians 4:32 (KJV)	and **be ye kind one to another,** tenderhearted, forgiving one another, even as God for Christ's sake hath forgiven you.
James 3:14-17 (KJV)	[14] But if ye have bitter envying and strife in your hearts, glory not, and lie not against the truth. [15] This wisdom descendeth not from above, but *is* earthly, sensual, devilish. [16] For where envying and strife *is,* there *is* confusion and every evil work. [17] But the wisdom that is from above is first pure, then peaceable, gentle, *and* easy to be intreated, full of mercy and good fruits, without partiality, and without hypocrisy.

27

As a White Christian, have you ever challenged any prejudices, racism, or bigotry expressed by others (relatives, friends, co-workers, business clients, church members, or leaders)? Why or why not?

_____

_____

_____

_____

How can you contribute to stopping the infectious spread of racism in the Church? In American society?

_____

_____

_____

_____

Do you recognize behaviors in America that are contrary to the Scriptures mentioned in this section that you have tolerated or excused (in yourself, in leadership, in politics)? List them. Have you renamed sowing disrespect and meanness as "boldness" for the sake of a vote?"

_____

_____

_____

IN CLOSING

- Racism has infiltrated and influenced many institutions, including the Christian Church.

- The Body of Christ is multicolored and multiracial. Yet the Church is overwhelmingly racially divided. God's vision for the Church is **UNITY** not division.

- Christians are the salt (the flavor) of the earth. But if salt has lost its savor (its voice), then it is good for nothing.

- At this point, the Church does not have a voice.

MATTHEW 5:13 (KJV)

[13]Ye are the **salt of the earth**: but if the salt have lost his savour, wherewith shall it be salted? it is thenceforth good for nothing, but to be cast out, and to be trodden under foot of men.

SELF-REFLECTION

Have you personally experienced or witnessed racism? How did you respond? Would God be pleased? What adjustments, if any, do you need to make?

_____

_____

_____

_____

_____

_____

Have you or your church, witnessed a distortion of Christianity that has condoned some form of racism? What can you do about this?

_____

_____

_____

_____

_____

_____

ONE ACTION

What is one thing that you can do that will help you to step outside of your comfort zone and practice what you have learned.

__Example:__ Think about your church. How does it rank in terms of diversity? What can you do to bring in people of other races and ethnicities?

__Example:__ How can you expose yourself to the teachings of other preachers or ministers of another race?

SESSION 3 – HISTORY MATTERS

POWER POINT:

In order to dismantle racism in the Church, a knowledge of the history of slavery in America must be discussed.

Slavery is a subject that many people find difficult to speak about. Some people experience many emotions like fear, anger, guilt, etc. at the mention of the word. Sometimes people often avoid discussions about it altogether.

THINKING EXPERIMENT: *When you hear the word "slavery" what thoughts or emotions come to your mind?*

_____

_____

_____

How would you define slavery? What do you think it means?

_____

_____

_____

WHAT WAS SLAVERY?

Slavery was a **SYSTEM**. It was deliberately structured to produce a **"plantation mentality."**

Slavery was designed by a racist mindset to create five (5) things:

1) A doctrine of inferiority
2) A sense of inadequacy
3) A negative self-concept
4) Dependency on the "White world"
5) Division of races and among races

In America, slavery was created to cause division between the White and Black race. Slavery also was created to cause those enslaved to become divided amongst themselves.

Slavery has generational impact. Does the impact of slavery continue to divide descendants of those who were enslaved? Have you been impacted? Please explain your answer.

_____

_____

_____

Of the five things that slavery created, explain any other generational consequences of slavery.

_____

_____

_____

WHAT IS GOD'S POSITION

What is your position on slavery?

_____

_____

_____

DID YOU KNOW? God has a clear position on slavery.

EXODUS 21:16 (KJV)	DEUTERONOMY 24:7 (KJV)
[16]And he that stealeth a man, and selleth him, or if he be found in his hand, he shall surely be put to death.	[7] If a man be found stealing any of his brethren of the children of Israel, and maketh merchandise of him, or selleth him; **then that thief shall die; and thou shalt put evil away from among you**.

God considers the act of stealing (kidnapping) and selling a human being as merchandise to be **thievery and evil**.

Looking back at your position on slavery is there a contradiction between your position and God's position? Are there any adjustments that you need to make? What are they?

_____

_____

_____

THE CO-CONSPIRACY

Genuine Christianity and the uncompromised preaching of God's Word presented a barrier to the justification of slavery and racial prejudice for slave owners and Christian missionaries. **They had to somehow quiet their consciences to engage in slavery.**

What in your life that you normally know is not "Christian-like" behavior, have you allowed your conscience to be quieted about?

_____

_____

_____

In order to tear down the barrier, there were two (2) tools used:

- The Tool of Legislation
- The Tool of the Bible

And in order to **dismantle racism in America**, the Tool of Legislation and the Tool of the Bible (genuine preaching of God's Word) must be applied.

THE TOOL OF LEGISLATION

There was an unwritten law in America that Christians could not be held as slaves.

If those who were enslaved (Black people) became Christians, this proposed a problem. Christian missionaries were motivating the slave owners to allow those enslaved to become Christians, but the enslavers were concerned about those enslaved being emancipated (freed, liberated) once they became a Christian.

To get around this dilemma, **laws** were enacted that stated that conversion (becoming a Christian) did not lead to a release of servitude (freedom).

Several laws were enforced against enslaved people. It was illegal for enslaved people to:

- read and write
- congregate
- own and sell property
- become citizens
- vote and hold office
- own firearms

In 1667, the Virginia General Assembly ENACTED A LAW that baptism and conversion to Christianity does not alter the condition of slaves nor release them of servitude.

Post-Civil War, Black Codes and Jim Crow laws further legalized discrimination, segregation, and racism in America.

For example, Jim Crow laws mandated the segregation of public schools, public places, and public transportation, and the segregation of restrooms, restaurants, and drinking fountains between White and Black people.

Do you have any friends or family members like grandparents or great grandparents that were victimized by the Tool of Legislation being used to legalize racism? What was the impact of their experience?

_____

_____

_____

Are there laws, policies, and procedures that you may be aware of on your job, in your church, or other places that favor one race over another? Name them. Who can you address them with to bring about change? What would you say?

_____

_____

_____

THE TOOL OF THE BIBLE

The Slave Bible was created and produced in England in 1807. It was a redacted version, meaning:

- All references to freedom, escape, and equality were removed.
- All references to submission and obedience to authority were kept.

In America, White preachers entered into a partnership with slave owners.

- They believed that preaching edited portions of the Bible would make enslaved people (Black people) better workers and serve as security against rebellion.

Slavery in America lasted for 246 years. It existed and persisted so long because White Christians sanctioned slavery and gave approval for enslavers.

POWER POINT:

If legislation and an edited, distorted version of the Bible justified and nailed down slavery into society, then **it would take both legislation and the uncompromised truth of the WHOLE Bible to lift slavery out of society**.

So, it is with racism, in America and in the Church. To dismantle racism, it will take BOTH legislation and the uncompromised teaching and preaching of the whole Word of God.

Can you think of a historical "fact" that you later learned was a myth created to preserve racism?

_____

_____

How can you contribute to dismantling racism in the church, on your job, at school, in your family? Write it down.

_____

_____

_____

Have you knowingly or unknowingly upheld any laws, policies, or procedures that support systemic racism? If yes, do you plan to change things? Please explain.

_____

_____

_____

WHITE CHRISTIANITY

Slavery gave birth to "White Christianity," which maintains the belief in both the inferiority of Black people and segregation.

In the United States, after the Civil War and in the north, formerly enslaved people could worship in the same church as White people but were relegated to segregated spaces. Black congregants had to

The division in the Body of Christ – the Black Church and the White Church – is a social construct and human invented class system. This was NOT God's intention.

sit in the balcony or in the back of the building and **they were never viewed as equal.** Consequently, they were not allowed to *integrate into leadership, integrate into participation, or integrate into freedom of expression.*

Hence the "Black Church" was birthed out of the unwillingness of White Christians to treat Black Christians as equals.

What are some consequences of the Christian Church being divided among races and people groups?

_____

_____

_____

Based on what you just learned concerning "White Christianity," do you think it is impacting the church today? Give examples.

_____

_____

_____

ANSWER HONESTLY: *Do you think a time is coming when worshipping across racial divides will be prevalent in the Church in America? Why or why not? What are your hopes for the future? Do you think everything is fine right now and require a change?*

_____

_____

_____

GENIUNE CHRISTIANITY

The infant Church in Paul's day was under the umbrella of Rome. Approximately 90% of the population in Rome were slaves. Slavery in Rome was different from slavery in America. In Rome, slavery was not about skin color, but about captives of war or indebtedness. The entire economy was built on slave labor. Instead of challenging the Church to revolt against slavery which would have destroyed the infant Church, **Paul attacked the institution of slavery at its spiritual roots.** Paul brought genuine Christianity to Rome and brought the uncompromised gospel to both the Christian enslavers and the enslaved. He attacked slavery by teaching the uncompromised Gospel and **unraveling the thread of slavery**.

If you want to remove a button from a garment, if you unravel enough threads, the whole garment will fall apart. The Bible provides insight on how to unravel the thread of slavery in America. These same insights can be leveraged to dismantle racism in the Church.

The Thread of Slavery	Bible Verse	The Gospel
Disrespect	**Ephesians 6:9** - And, **ye masters, do the same things unto them,** forbearing threatening: knowing that your Master also is in heaven; neither is there respect of persons with him.	**Respect** (mutual)
Harsh Treatment	**Ephesians 6:9** - And, ye masters, do the same things unto them, **forbearing threatening:** knowing that your Master also is in heaven; neither is there respect of persons with him.	**Kindness** (forbear threatening)
Superiority	**Ephesians 6:9** - And, ye masters, do the same things unto them, forbearing threatening: knowing that your Master also is in heaven; **neither is there respect of persons with him**.	**Impartiality** (God doesn't put one above another)
Inequality	**Galatians 3:28** - There is neither Jew nor Greek, there is neither bond nor free, there is neither male nor female: **for ye are all one** in Christ Jesus	**Equality**

The Thread of Slavery	Bible Verse	The Gospel
Unfair Treatment	**Colossians 4:1 -** Masters, **give unto *your* servants that which is just and equal;** knowing that ye also have a Master in heaven.	**Fairness/ Justice**
Non-personhood	**Philemon 15-16 -** For perhaps he therefore departed for a season, that thou shouldest receive him for ever; **not now as a servant, but above a servant, a brother beloved,** specially to me, but how much more unto thee, both in the flesh, and in the Lord?	**True Brotherhood**

Have you ever witnessed, participated in, or experienced any of the threads of racism? How have these Bible insights impacted your beliefs about racism?

_____

_____

POWER POINT:

Christianity fully embraced and lived out = EQUALITY

IN CLOSING

Racism is still alive and well in America and prevalent in the Church. In order to dismantle racism, the Tool of Legislation and Tool of the Bible, genuine teaching and preaching of God's Word must be **applied.**

SELF-REFLECTION

Have you intentionally sought out experiences, information, or resources that helped you learn more about people of different races? What have you discovered about yourself and others?

_____

_____

_____

ONE ACTION

What is one thing that you can do that will help you to step outside of your comfort zone and practice what you've learned?

Example(s):

- *Memorize at least one Scripture that embraces God's heart on equality.*
- *Visit a church that is predominantly another race than your own.*
- *If you see harsh treatment, step in and do something.*
- *If you see or hear about an injustice, name it as an injustice.*
- *Create a social media post announcing your new mindset.*

SESSION 4- HISTORY MATTERS: PRESENT-DAY REALITIES

POWER POINT:

Slavery, racism, and racial injustice are topics that many people are uncomfortable speaking about. However, no matter how uncomfortable it is, these discussions are necessary to bring about racial equality and reconciliation.

Undoing racism is not a quick fix. So that one may have deep, honest, open, relevant, and transformative discussions to move forward and to bring about change, **a knowledge of history is imperative**. There must be intentionality about studying, learning, and getting information to bridge the knowledge gap. Simply said, **History Matters.**

Keep the following themes in mind when reviewing and studying the topics in this session:

Session Themes	**Accountability** - to hold responsible for actions. • Accountability creates trust and support. • Lack of accountability erodes trust and destroys trust. **Psychological Vestiges** – traces of our past often show up in our present. • Traces from the past that are evident in the present, and apart from interruption, will be evident in the future. **Consequences** – Whenever seeds are sown, there are consequences. • We reap what we sow. • Galatians 6:7-8 (MSG) - [7-8] Don't be misled: No one makes a fool of God. What a person plants, he will harvest. **The person who plants selfishness, ignoring the needs of others — ignoring God! — harvests a crop of weeds**…

How can a lack of knowledge hinder successful discussions about racism?

_____

_____

_____

What is the impact of engaging in conversations about racism without a knowledge of history?

_____

_____

_____

BLACK SELF-HATE

The word "hate" is a strong word. Have you ever stopped to think about how often the word is used? We all use it. We say things like, "I hate that song", "I hate a certain food", "I hate my job." In that context the word hate does not sound so bad. But what about when the word is used towards another person - **I HATE YOU** or even worse **I HATE MYSELF**?

Black self-hate is a "**plantation mentality**." The following chart identifies the origin of Black self-hate and the generational impact in our present day. Please note the realities listed do not apply to ALL Black people. Also notice the psychological vestiges that have flowed through history into our present reality.

American Slavery	Present-Day Realities
Slavery programmed enslaved males to be irresponsible.	More than 70% of African American children are raised by single parents.
Enslaved males were studs, whose job was to make enslaved babies and enslaved women were treated as sex objects.	Some Black men are still acting like studs by not forming lasting relationships and Black women are treated as sexual objects (Ex. movies, videos).
Enslaved people were taught to devalue Black life.	Black on Black crime
Lighter skinned enslaved people with features closer to the enslaver were treated better.	Beauty is still based on color of skin, hair texture and facial features (i.e. colorism).
Slaves were discouraged from uniting. They were rewarded for snitching. They were pitted against one another (light-skinned vs. dark-skinned; house slaves vs. field slaves). **Note:** White people called Black people the N-word. House n***** / Field n*****	Some Black people struggle working with other Black people; Black people talking against other successful Black people due to jealousy; Goods and services created by Black people are believed (by other Black people) to be inferior. **Note**: These things are true even among Christians (Plantation Mentality).
During slavery, it was best to blend in; literacy and intelligence were outlawed.	Black kids ridicule other Black kids for being smart.
In slavery time, enslaved people were given the worst food and leftovers.	Some Black movie producers, music producers, and comedians give Black people a lot of **plantation food**. (Metaphorically, plantation food is perpetuated in music and movies— packed with destructive themes like profanity and sex exploitation, rather than themes of inspiration.)

How does the word "hate" make you feel?

_____

_____

_____

Have you ever felt hate toward yourself or others? Why? Describe those feelings.

_____

_____

_____

What can you do to channel any negative feelings you may have?

_____

_____

_____

If you are a Black person, think about your own life, does Black self-hate manifest itself in your life? If yes, give examples.

_____

_____

_____

- *What can you do to change it?*

    _____

    _____

- *What can you do to change the present-day realities in your family and community?*

    _____

    _____

    _____

PLANTATION MENTALITY IN A WORD: THE N-WORD

What does the "N" word mean to you?

_____

_____

_____

The plantation mentality can be summarized in ONE WORD. The "N" word is the most racially offensive word toward Black people in the history of America.

The "N" word was used by enslavers to insult, injure and distinguished White people from Black people. This racial slur was used to communicate that Black people were innately ignorant, uncivilized, and an inferior race of being (not human).

An understanding of the origin of the "N" word should eradicate it from your vocabulary.

Black self-hate occurs when Black people believe and accept the negative persona that has been given to them by the world. As a race and as individuals, Black people must reject the negative view of themselves and turn their attention to what God says about them in His Word.

Having the proper perspective of themselves, and respecting and loving themselves will also help them to have the proper perspective of others. It begins on the inside.

Because of its origin in history, Black people should **NEVER** use the "N" word to refer to themselves. It is important that everyone hold themselves accountable to how they treat themselves as well as others.

POWER POINT:

The Word of God commands to love your neighbor as yourselves. Love begins on the inside. It is important for everyone to respect, love, accept themselves and to see themselves the way God sees them.

Do you see the "N" word as a present-day vestige of American slavery?

_____

Have you ever used the "N" word? If yes, explain why you used it?

_____

_____

_____

When you hear the "N" word what emotions do you experience?

_____

_____

_____

LOOTING

Looting means:

- **Sack** – to rob of valuables after capture
- **Despoil** – to strip of belongings—things that belong to others
- **Remove** – take things away by force

POWER POINT:

Protesting and looting are NOT the same thing. The two words should not be confused.

Thousands of people have taken to the streets nationally and internationally in protests to denounce institutional racism and police violence after George Floyd was murdered when a police officer knelt on his neck for 8 minutes.

But the breaking of windows, burning of property, breaking into stores, and stealing of goods that have distracted from the generally, peaceful demonstrations have been disheartening. Honest, caring people, no matter the race, struggle with looting. People who loot should be held accountable. The problem with looting is that it changes the narrative. It moves the narrative from change to "unrest" and undermines future progress.

How does looting undermine progress?

_____

_____

_____

WHITE FOLK LOOTING

White people have looted the belongings of Black people (biblical history, world history, and American history).

HELPFUL INFO

The purpose of this section is not to get White individuals to feel guilty about the looting of history. Each White person did NOT personally rob Black people of their biblical, World, and American history. The purpose is to inform you, so you are aware of this generational and systemic racism, and **at the very least**, can have empathy.

BIBLICAL HISTORY

Many people have not heard about Black people in Scripture because White people looted biblical history from black people.

There are Black people represented in the Old and New Testament. The chart below represents Black people in the Bible.

Biblical Black Person	Scripture	Description
Nimrod	Genesis 10	He was a brilliant empire builder. He built the City of Babylon.
Jethro	Exodus 19	He was Moses' father-in-law, mentor, and counselor.
Hobab	Numbers 10	He was Jethro's son; he was Moses' scout through the wilderness.
Queen of Sheba	1 Kings 10	She was a Black queen.
Zephaniah	Zephaniah	He received the Word of the Lord and wrote Zephaniah, an Old Testament book. He was of Hamitic origin, having descended from the line of Cush. Cush was one of Ham's sons and Ham was the father of the Black race.

Biblical Black Person	Scripture	Description
--	--	Abraham, Moses, and Joseph married Black women.
Simon of Cyrene	Mark 15	He helped bear Jesus' cross.
Alexander and Rufus	Mark 15; Romans 16	They were the sons of Simon of Cyrene.
Ethiopian Eunuch	Acts 8	He was a man of great authority under the Queen of Ethiopia.
Simeon, called Niger	Acts 13	He was a prophet or teacher in the first Christian church at Antioch, which was a multiracial, multi-cultural Church with Blacks in leadership.
Lucius of Cyrene	Acts 13	He was a prophet or teacher in the first Christian church at Antioch, which was a multiracial, multi-cultural Church with Blacks in leadership.
Simon, the Canaanite	Matthew 10	He was one of the twelve disciples. He was a descendant of Ham.

How does knowledge about accurate biblical history help to erode Black self-hate?

_____

_____

_____

Describe how accurate biblical history challenges the myth of Black inferiority?

_____

_____

_____

Does your church teach about Black people in the Bible? If not, what could you do to change this?

_____

_____

_____

If you are a pastor, minister, church leader, volunteer, or small group leader, could you pledge to incorporate these positive biblical references of Black people as an ongoing commitment to help break the cycle of negative racial and ethnic socialization (RES)? If not, please explain.

_____

_____

_____

WORLD HISTORY

In World History class, students are not taught about Black people's ancient civilizations and their extensive contributions. And many times, their achievements are attributed to other racial groups. **Their contributions in world history are unknown by many because White people looted the history.** In the United States, the public have been told that Black people were uncivilized, ignorant, and incapable of learning and leading. However, nothing could be further from the truth.

When you look at world history, you should consider these historical facts:

- Ancient Egypt was known as the Land of Ham, the father of the Black race. (Psalm 105:23)
- Descendants of Ham (people of color, Black people) ruled most of the known world for the first 2000 years of world history. They were the most advanced people on the earth, building empires, organizing governments.
- Ancient Egyptians were people of color who were proficient in mathematics, medicine, engineering, and architecture (e.g. great pyramids)
- People of color gave the world what has been known as modern calculus.

Why do you think these facts are not widely known and/or discussed? Does institutional racism play a role? Please explain.

_____

_____

_____

If accurate world history were common knowledge, how would that impact racism in America? How would it impact the Church?

_____

_____

_____

How does knowing this information impact you? Please explain.

_____

_____

_____

If knowing this information has impacted you, has it changed your perspective any? If so, in what ways?

_____

_____

_____

Describe how accurate world history challenges the myth of Black inferiority.

_____

_____

_____

AMERICAN HISTORY

Before the Civil War (1861-1865), enslavement was legal in the United States. Enslaved people were considered property and could not apply for patents. That did not stop them from creating new inventions though. **Black people's achievements in American history are unknown by many because White people looted the history.** In American History classes, students are given a skewed view of Black people's American history. They are consistently taught about slavery (which perpetuates White superiority and Black inferiority) without teaching about Black people's significant, widespread contributions across various industries. Many times, inventions are credited to White people. Some of the world's most popular inventions were created by Black people. There were many Black people, men and women, enslaved and free, who contributed (and are still contributing) in a big way to American history.

INVENTION	BLACK INVENTOR
Portable Refrigeration System for trucks	Frederick McKinley Jones
Clothes Dryer	George T. Sampson
Automatic Gear Shift	Richard Spikes
Fire Extinguisher	Thomas J. Martin
Dry Cleaning	Thomas Jenny
Gas Mask	Garret Morgan
Modern Lawn Mower	L.A. Burr
Blood Banks	Dr. Charles Richard Drew
Automatic Opening and Closing Elevator Door	Alexander Miles
Laserphaco Probe and Cataract Surgery Procedure	Dr. Patricia Bath
Hundreds of Uses of the Peanut	George Washington Carver
Pioneer of Open-Heart Surgery	Daniel Hale Williams

Other great names are Oscar Charleston, Josh Gibson, John Henry Lloyd, Cool Papa Bell, Buck Leonard. Many people have never heard of them. They were baseball players who could only play in the Negro League. **They are not in the record books because they were banned from Major League Baseball.** American history is INCOMPLETE.

Why would someone intentionally omit information about the role of Black people from America's history?

_____

_____

_____

What harm can result from erasing or leaving out the historical contributions of Black people from American history?

_____

_____

_____

How has this information impacted you? What are your thoughts and feelings?

_____

_____

_____

How do you think having an accurate knowledge of American history can impact racism in America?

_____

_____

_____

What can be done to ensure that people have a complete view of American history?

_____

_____

_____

DOG WHISTLE POLITICS

According to Ephesians 4:3, we are to labor to keep peace, the unity of the spirit in the bond of peace. **It is important for ALL Christians to labor to keep peace.** As we navigate through the political world it is critical for us to see anything that divides us.

POWER POINT:

Coded language does the opposite of keeping the peace, it causes division.

Coded Language - {def} expressing ambiguous and hidden messages and opinions about race in an indirect way to speak to some without offending others (Ex. dog whistle)

Dog Whistle Politics is:

- clandestinely soliciting and rallying certain people using certain phrases that resonate with that target audience.
- coded racist appeals.
- a political strategy, set of statements, appeals, or slogans that conveys a controversial secondary message which is only understood by those who support the message.

According to Merriam Webster Dictionary:

Figuratively, a 'dog' whistle' is a coded message communicated through words or phrases commonly understood by a particular group of people, but not by others.

FOR EXAMPLE

o   When you hear "law and order" from a politician, what does that mean and who is the target audience?

o   When you hear "war on drugs," what does that mean and who is the target audience?

o   When you hear "war on terror", what does that mean? Do you think about those of Arab or Muslim descent?

o   What do you think when you hear, "Make America Great Again?" What did we lose that we need to get back? Some interpret this as a dog whistle that is interpreted as a Whiter, more Anglo-Saxon past. Some see this as coded language designed to signal a rollback to a time when people of color and women knew their place.

o   What did President Donald Trump mean when he told a White Supremist group to "stand back and standby" on live national television when he was asked to denounce White Supremacy? Was this a mistake? Or was this a dog whistle?

THE CONFEDERACY

CONFEDERATE FLAGS AND MONUMENTS

There have been debates in America about the removal of Confederate flags, statues, monuments, names from streets, and names from college buildings. Some people think it is very important to remove these things, others do not.

- NASCAR banned the Confederate flag. *Why did they ban it?*
- The State of Mississippi retired a State Flag that had Confederate emblems on it. *Why did they think this was important?*

Some people believe that the Confederate flags, statues, and monuments represent service, the preservation of American heritage, and southern values. Other people think that the Confederate symbols represent the ownership of enslaved people and reinforce concepts of the superiority of the White race and the inferiority of the Black race, which causes division.

> **POWER POINT:**
>
> We, as Christians, CANNOT allow ourselves to cause division.

If we are going to have conversations about the flags and monuments, it is important for you to be equipped with information. The chart below provides this information.

HISTORY HUDDLE – THE CONFEDERATE CAUSE

DID YOU KNOW?

o   The Confederacy (or the Confederate States of America) was a collection of eleven states that seceded, or broke away, from the U.S. in 1860 following the election of Abraham Lincoln.

o   The Confederacy was convinced that White supremacy and the institution of slavery was threatened by the election of Abraham Lincoln.

o   The Confederate President, Jefferson Davis, said that America was founded by White men for White men.

o   In the "Cornerstone Address," the Confederacy Vice President, Alexander H. Stephens said, "upon the great truth that the Negro is not equal to the White man, that slavery, subordination to the superior race is his, the Black man's, natural and normal condition."

o   Alexander H. Stephens said that the Confederacy went to war (the Civil War - ultimately killing 600,000 to 800,000 people) in order to "protect our property" (referring to enslaved people). Some people say the Civil War was fought for "states' rights." However, specifically it was concerning the states' rights to own slaves, who they depended on for their livelihood.

o   The Confederacy was a repressive, pro-slavery nation devoted to White supremacy and a nation that was at war against the United States.

The purpose of Confederate statues, flags, and names was to preserve the memory of the Confederate cause and the people who fought and died for that cause.

What thoughts and emotions come to mind upon discovering the cause of the Confederacy?

_____

_____

_____

What are your thoughts on the removal of Confederate statues, flags, and monuments?

_____

_____

_____

When considering the cause of the Confederacy, how does advocating for preservation of Confederate monuments contradict the basic tenets of Christianity? How do you think Jesus would have responded to the cause of the Confederacy?

_____

_____

_____

_____

_____

Would Confederate monuments be better served inside of a Civil War museum instead of displayed in a town square? Why or why not?

_____

_____

_____

IN CLOSING

In order to have honest, open, and transformative discussions to move forward and bring about change, an accurate knowledge of HISTORY is imperative. There must be intentionality about bridging the knowledge gap.

SELF-REFLECTION

After reviewing the content in this session, how would you describe your comfort level regarding your ability to discuss your thoughts and opinions of these topics with others?

Very comfortable	Somewhat comfortable	Not comfortable

What lingering questions do you have? What can you do to get those questions answered and become more comfortable with having meaningful conversations with others?

_____

_____

_____

Example(s):

- *Join a Small Group*
- *Watch the entire 7-episode Muted Voice docuseries (FREE at www.mutedvoice.info)*
- *Reread this Study Guide*
  - *Perform your own in-depth study of the biblical references*

ONE ACTION

What is one thing that you can do that will help you to step outside of your comfort zone and practice what you've learned?

Example(s):

- *Read books about Black Americans to gain more insight.*
- *Host a showing and discussion of the movie **Hidden Figures**.*
- *Suggest books for libraries, bookstores, and even schools on Black American History.*
- *Share what you have learned with your family, friends, and community.*

SESSION 5 – THE UNMUTED VOICE

SILENCE IS COMPLICIT

The Civil Rights Leader, Dr. Martin Luther King, Jr. said, "Our lives begin to end the day we become **silent** about things that matter." "In the end, we will remember not the words of our enemies, but the **silence** of our friends."

How do you interpret this quote?

_____

_____

_____

It has been said that our strongest tool against terrorism is "see something, say something." This tool is equally effective when it comes to matters of racism and racial injustice. It is up to each of us to say something, to speak out about racism and racial injustice.

Complicit means to be involved with others in an illegal activity or to be involved with others in a wrongdoing.

POWER POINT:

Silent complicity – being silent or inactive in the face of systemic or continuous human rights abuse.

To be silent is to be complicit. To be complicit is a form of passive racism.

Is there damage that occurs when there's silent complicity? Please explain.

_____

_____

_____

Consider this illustration of passive racism:

Psychologist Beverly Daniel Tatum said, regarding the system of racism, "I sometimes visualize the ongoing cycle of racism as a moving walkway at the airport. ***Active racist*** behavior is equivalent to walking fast on the conveyer belt. ***Passive racist*** behavior is equivalent to standing still on the walkway. No overt effort is being made but the conveyer belt moves the bystander along to the same destination as those who are actively walking."

What are your thoughts about this statement?

_____

_____

_____

Have you or someone you know ever engaged in active or passive racist behavior? Give an example. What was the outcome?

_____

_____

_____

THE SIGNIFICANCE OF PREACHING AGAINST RACISM

Ministers of the Gospel (Pastors, Evangelists, Prophets, Apostles, Teachers) play a key role in unmuting the voice of the Church by intentionally speaking out against racism. If you are a minister of the Gospel, this section is for you.

Racism is:

- A generational curse that must be broken
- A demonic spirit of division
- A mental stronghold established over time, fortified by customs, and resistant to change

To ministers, this means that general teaching on love, generosity, and service alone will **not break the power of a spiritual demonic force**. Some spirits, like racism cannot be side-stepped. It must be directly confronted. The only thing that will break the power of racism over the **Church is the preaching of the Gospel.** You must preach it!

PREACHING AND SALVATION

ROMANS 1:16 (KJV)

[16] For I am not ashamed of the gospel of Christ: for it is the power of God unto salvation to every one that believeth; to the Jew first, and also to the Greek.

As you read this Scripture, notice the gospel of Christ is the power of God unto salvation to everyone who believes. **Salvation means deliverance, wholeness, healing, restoration, and provision.** IT MEANS TO BE SAVED.

Why is the preaching of the Gospel important to break the power of racism in the Church?

_____

_____

_____

What steps has your church taken to helped dismantle racism?

_____

_____

_____

_____

_____

Did you ever think of racism as a demonic spiritual force, a spirit of division? Explain.

_____

_____

_____

PREACHING AND FAITH

ROMANS 10:13-14, 17 (KJV)

[13] For whosoever shall call upon the name of the Lord shall be saved. [14] How then shall they call on him in whom they have not believed? and how shall they believe in him of whom they have not heard? and how shall they hear without a preacher? [17] **So then faith** *cometh* **by hearing, and hearing by the word of God**.

Faith for deliverance in any area (sins, addictions, etc.) comes by hearing God's Word. Faith for deliverance from **racism** comes by hearing God's Word. Hearing God's Word is like a superpower. It is remarkably effective and powerful!

POWER POINT:

It is an unrealistic expectation for a pastor to think that his or her church members will be delivered from **racism** without hearing the truth of the Gospel.

Do you agree or disagree with the power point? Please explain.

_____

_____

_____

MINISTERS OF THE GOSPEL MUST TEACH ON RACISM IN THE CHURCH

The Church has a major role in bringing racial reconciliation. Every minister (pastor, evangelists, prophet, apostle, teacher) has the responsibility to preach and teach on racism.

TO THE BLACK MINISTER (PASTOR)

Black ministers have a responsibility to preach and teach clear, specific, and biblical lessons on race, racism, and racial reconciliation.

Some Black Christians may have experienced racism directly or indirectly and it is possible some members of your congregation may have emotions about race that may not be constructive or wholesome. Some may even be dealing with prejudice. In sharing the Word of God to them, be sure to include Ephesians 4:26 (KJV). It says to "be ye angry, and sin not: let not the sun go down upon your wrath." They are Black people with a Black frame of reference, with a Black worldview, that have a Black experience, living in a White-led America. As a result, there may also be members who are dealing with inferiority. You must speak out!

Your anointed teaching helps in 3 ways:

- Aids and guides Black Christians in properly processing their emotions in constructive ways
- Breaks the power of reactionary racism
- Destroys any stronghold of "inferiority"

TO THE WHITE MINISTER (PASTOR)

White ministers must preach and teach clear, specific, and biblical lessons on race, racism, and racial reconciliation. It may be uncomfortable, but you are called to preach God's Word to bring a deliverance.

Although you may have zero issues in your heart concerning racism, you cannot say the same thing about everyone in your congregation. Some White Christians in your congregation may have blind spots concerning race, racial equality, and injustice. They are White people with a White frame of reference, with a White worldview, that have a White experience, living in a White-led America. As a result, some may be involved in, operate in, and participate in generational racism, and have issues of superiority that need deliverance. You must speak out against this!

Consider this: If you do not teach on subjects like evangelism and leading others to Christ, your church members will not feel comfortable evangelizing because they do not have the knowledge base to do so. In the same way, if there is no preaching and teaching on racial matters, then your members will not feel comfortable participating in open and honest dialogue without defensiveness.

Your anointed teaching helps in 3 ways:

- Aids and motivates White Christians to be open and participate in honest and transparent discussions on race and racism without defensiveness
- Breaks the power of generational racism
- Destroys any stronghold of "superiority"

POWER POINT:

No pastor, no matter the color, can say that ALL members of their congregation do not deal with issues of racism. That is why **NOT** teaching on racial matters **IS NOT AN OPTION**; it is a topic that must be addressed.

Why is it important to integrate teaching about racism into the Church? What are the challenges? What are the benefits?

_____

_____

_____

_____

_____

If you are a minister of the Gospel, what surprises you about your beliefs on racism?

_____

_____

_____

If you are a minister, you understand the power of the Gospel. Is teaching on race, racial reconciliation, or race relations part of your teaching curriculum? Yes or no? Why or why not?

_____

_____

_____

_____

Are there any actions you need to take that would help you to teach effectively on racism?

_____

_____

_____

_____

CHRISTIANITY AS A BRAND IS NOT THE ANSWER

Do you have a favorite cereal? What brand is it? Think about Kellogg's. Kellogg's has many different brands of cereal: Fruit Loops, Frosted Flakes, Raisin Bran, Rice Krispies.

In the Church in America today, it is unfortunate that in many cases, we have Christianity as a brand. Branded Christianity, which is a politicized version of Christianity, embraces some parts of the Bible and excludes, edits, or dismisses other parts of the Bible. **The entire Word of God is the answer, not just parts of it.**

Believers can register under any party affiliation that they choose or are led to connect with, and they can even be and should be active in politics. **But they should NOT identify Christianity or the Church with a political party.**

REPUBLICAN PARTY	DEMOCRATIC PARTY

• Many White evangelical ministers and leaders believe and communicate that the Republican party is [the] party for committed Christians.
 	
 • They highlight the Republican party's platform and opposition on abortion and same-sex marriage and how these positions line up with Scripture.
 	
 • The Republican party leans more toward the biblical view of the right-to-life of the unborn and heterosexual marriage.
 	
 • The Republican party and many White evangelical ministers are silent on the issues of racism and racial equality.
 	
 • Many believe:
   ○ There is no systemic racism
   ○ There is no White privilege
	• The Democratic party's platform and position is often associated with social justice, racial equality, and equal opportunity.
	
	 • The Democratic party leans more towards the biblical command to lift the poor and defend the rights of the oppressed:
	
	   ○ *"He gave **justice** and **help** to the poor and needy and everything went well with him. Isn't that what it means to know me says the Lord."* – **Jeremiah 22:16 NLT**
	
	   ○ NOTE: Many Republicans, on the other hand, believe too much aid to the poor is **socialism**.
	
	   ○ God's attitude towards racism is that He is no respecter of persons (Acts 10:34-35).
	
	     ▪ Racism is a sin.
	
	     ▪ Racism kills people, dreams, accomplishments, motivation, potential, and **unity**.

The problem with Branded Christianity is that it:

- Causes Christians to fall from having a **voice** to becoming a **vote**. God did not create the Church to be a VOTE. God gave the Church a VOICE to the world.
- Embraces some parts of the Bible and excludes, ignores, or edits other parts of the Bible.
- Causes division, which is unbiblical
- Causes the Gospel to be tied to a political party, candidate, or politician. Jesus is above all parties. In Christ, there is neither conservative nor liberal, right nor left. We are ONE in Christ.

When you read the section on Branded Christianity, did any feelings arise? If so, what were they?

_____

_____

_____

What thoughts and feelings come to mind when you observe the belief system of the Republican party? The Democratic Party?

_____

_____

_____

*What aspects of both parties align with your personal belief system? What aspects of **both** parties align with Christianity?*

_____

_____

_____

What criteria should Christians use when contemplating their voting strategy?

_____

_____

71

Why can't revival in America occur until racism is broken over the Church?

_____

_____

_____

Do you think that racial discrimination was resolved during the Civil Rights Movement and evidenced by the presidency of President Barack Obama? Explain.

_____

_____

_____

Every party wants Jesus on their side, but Jesus is not a Republican, Democrat, or Independent.

- *Why should the Gospel never be tied to a party, a candidate, or a politician?*

    _____

    _____

    _____

- *In your own words, describe how Branded Christianity causes Christians to fall from having a "voice" to a "vote."*

    _____

    _____

    _____

- *How is associating the Church and Christianity with a party inherently divisive?*

    _____

    _____

    _____

SELECTIVE MUTISM

Branded Christianity can lead to a form of *selective mutism*. Selective mutism is a severe anxiety disorder that prevents people from speaking in certain social situations while being able to communicate effectively in other settings and situations in which they feel more comfortable, supported, and secure.

When Christianity is politicized, people may see things that they know go against fundamental Christian values (love, joy, peace, patience, kindness, goodness, faithfulness, gentleness, self-control), but they will not say anything even when they know it is wrong.

How do you think Branded Christianity has caused selective mutism in yourself or others? Why or why not?

_____

_____

_____

As a Believer, have you found that you have wanted to speak out against wrongs that you have seen within your own political party, but you allowed your voice to be muted because you feared the reaction of others that you were not being loyal? Explain.

_____

_____

_____

_____

_____

Have you told yourself that it is permissible for you to call people names and be mean (in person, via text, on social media, and/or in your church) because they are associated with a political party or belief system different than yours? Explain.

_____

_____

_____

_____

_____

_____

IN CLOSING

- Ministers of the Gospel **must** preach and teach the uncompromised Word of God as it relates to race, racism, racial reconciliation, and racial equality to bring faith and deliverance to the Body of Christ. What brings people out of the darkness is the teaching of the whole Gospel. Ministers must speak out!

- Racism is the *number one thing* that is standing in between America and the Church having revival. Revival cannot occur until racism is broken over the Church.

- Christians should NOT identify Christianity or the Church with a political party. Christianity as a brand is not the answer.

SELF-REFLECTION

On a scale from 0 to 5, with 0 being "no" and 5 being the highest score, have you been complicit on matters of racism? Explain why you gave yourself this score.

_____

_____

_____

- *Is there room for improvement? If so, how? (Be open to try.)*

_____

_____

_____

_____

ONE ACTION

What is one thing that you can do that will help you to step outside of your comfort zone and practice what you have learned?

How will you use your voice to speak out against racial injustice?

Example(s):

- *Write social media posts*
- *Lead or participate in a small group*
- *Host a "Lunch and Learn"*
- *Teach it at your church*
- *Text friends and family*
- *Forward the Muted Voice Docuseries to a friend*

SESSION 6 – WHY SOME WHITE PEOPLE STRUGGLE TALKING ABOUT RACISM

"The best things in life are on the other side of a difficult conversation. If we can have the conversation in a better way, we can make meaningful change in the world around us."

~ Kwame Christian, Esq., M.A.

Do you agree with this statement? Why or why not?

_____

_____

_____

People struggle talking about racism because of roadblocks. Overcoming the hurdles and roadblocks of **blind spots**, *a lack of empathy*, and **denial** is essential to having open, honest, and transparent communication about racism in general and specifically in the Church.

POWER POINT:

Conversations on "racism" are difficult, but they are necessary.

BLIND SPOTS

We have all heard of blind spots when driving. Blind spots are any area where your view is obstructed. An object or person could be right next to your vehicle even though you do not realize it. However, someone viewing from a different vantage point can see clearly. And although you cannot see it, this does not eliminate the real dangers.

Research indicates that everyone has blind spots. The danger with blind spots on racism is that it can hinder racial reconciliation. No one is exempt from blind spots. We can see them in others, but are we aware of our own?

A **blind spot** is:

- A gap in a person's perceptions that blinds them from seeing the truth in themselves or in others.
  - In Matthew 7:5 (NKJV), Jesus said, "first remove the plank from your own eye, **and then you will see clearly** to remove the speck from your brother's eye." (This means there is something in our own eye that keeps us from seeing clearly — a **blind spot.**)

- A complete lack of insight as how one's behavior is affecting others.
  - The refusal to listen, defensiveness, anger, and justification have a negative impact and can shut down the conversation.

Do you believe that everyone (including yourself) has blind spots? Please explain.

_____

_____

_____

What are some ways you can recognize your blind spots?

_____

_____

_____

Do you have anyone in your life who has a different vantage point, who you can be accountable to, to help you recognize and work on overcoming your blind spots concerning race relations? Who are they?

_____

People can have blind spots, be sincere, not intend to be insensitive, and at the same time be insensitive. How can you personally prevent this from happening? How can you help others do the same?

_____

_____

_____

_____

Why do you think defensiveness, anger, and justification can shut down effective conversations on racism?

_____

_____

_____

Have you ever gotten defensive and angry when conversing on matters of race?

_____

_____

_____

- *What was the outcome? What could you do differently?*

    _____

    _____

    _____

Tips for Removing Blind Spots	
Prayer	• Ask God to search, evaluate, and provide feedback on you and your motives. • Ask God to make your motives clear to you. • Evaluate yourself as you are spending time with God. • **Ask God to reveal yourself to you.** • Melt before the truth, by acknowledging what you discover from God to be true. • Ask for and depend upon the grace of God for transformation.
Feedback	• Embrace feedback from an outsider. NOTE: We all need someone to tell us the truth even at the expense of hurting our feelings • Be willing to listen to what you learn. • Commit actions of change based on what you learn about yourself from outsiders.

LACK OF EMPATHY

People also struggle having conversations on racism because of a **lack of empathy**. Empathy is the ability to relate to the thoughts, emotions, and experiences of others. Whenever people express concern and show that they understand, it creates a connection. When people are indifferent, it drives a wedge.

SCRIPTURAL EMPATHY

ROMANS 12:15 (NLT)

[15]Be happy with those who are happy, and weep with those who weep.

THREE DISTINCT KINDS OF EMPATHY	
Emotional Empathy	The ability to feel what someone else feels.
Cognitive Empathy	The ability to understand another person's perspective.
Empathic Concern	The ability to sense what another person needs from you.

LACK OF EMPATHY ILLUSTRATION:

When a White person makes a statement that the "playing field is level" and that "all a Black person needs to do is work hard," shows a lack of empathy. Why does this show a lack of empathy? It conveys a lack of knowledge on the reason there is a gap and a disability to understand another person's perspective. Enslavement, unfair systemic policies and laws (banking, employment, education, entertainment), Jim Crow laws, Black codes, voter suppression, segregation, housing discrimination, racial profiling, and the gap in wealth opportunities, do not make the playing field level.

Based on the distinct kinds of empathy described, explain how this illustration is a lack of empathy.

_____

_____

_____

BONUS: This illustration also demonstrates a blind spot as well. Did you recognize it? _____

EMPATHY ILLUSTRATION:

A Black protestor was peacefully kneeling several yards away from and facing a line of police in full protective gear. A White protestor went and kneeled directly in front of the Black protestor. Later, a reporter asked the White protestor was he afraid kneeling in front of the Black protestor and he answered, "no." When asked why, he said, "*because I am White*."

Based on the distinct kinds of empathy described above, explain how this illustration is an example of empathy.

_____

_____

_____

Do you believe as a Christian, and having the nature of Jesus Christ in you, you should feel any empathy towards racial inequalities?

_____

Does it upset you when someone outside of your race is treated disrespectfully or mistreated? Why or why not?

_____

_____

_____

Think of instances where you thought a person was being mistreated, were they all people within your own race? Or was there a mixture of people from various races and cultures?

_____

_____

POWER POINT:

In Matthew 9:36, Jesus saw the crowds and was moved with compassion. Empathy leads to compassion and it motivates people to action.

DENIAL OF SYSTEMIC RACISM

Some White Christians are in denial of systemic racism. They believe that it does not exist.

Denial is a roadblock to the conversation on racism. It is a refusal to believe or accept something as the truth.

The root of denial is:

- Some White people view life from a White point of reference, White worldview, and a White experience.

- It is easy to be in denial when you do not have a point of reference. Some White people believe the Black experience is the same as their own experience. However, it is vastly different.

REVELATION 3:17, 18B (CEV)

[17]You claim to be rich and successful and to have everything you need. But you don't know how bad off you are. You are pitiful, poor, blind, and naked… [18B]Buy medicine for your eyes, so that you will be able to see.

*Have you **truly listened** to others who have a different point of reference and a different world view and experience to see what their experiences are?*

_____

_____

DENIAL OF WHITE PRIVILEGE

Denial of White privilege can be roadblock to the conversation on race relations. Recognizing "**White privilege**" begins with an understanding of what it means.

What "White privilege" is not:

- ✓ White privilege does not suggest that all White people are wealthy and have never struggled in life or life was easy growing up.

- ✓ It is "NOT" the assumption that everything a White person has accomplished is unearned. Hard work and sacrifice to achieve their level of success is the outcome for many.

- ✓ Having White privilege or even recognizing that they have it, does not mean that White people are racist or that they have personally cheated others to obtain what they possess.

Why do you think some people deny White privilege? Do you?

_____

_____

_____

What is White Privilege?

Frances E Kendall said, "White privilege is having greater access to power and resources than people of color **in the same situation**.

Cory Collins says, "White privilege is a legacy!"

- White status and citizenship brought certain advantages.
- Historically, being white was required to be a citizen of the U.S.
- Historically, being black brought certain disadvantages

> Black people could not….

> - Vote
> - Hold a public office or position
> - Own personal or intellectual property
> - Have a stable personal or family life
> - Have a business or be self-employed

White privilege is a built-in advantage separate from the level of income, effort, and talent.

Illustrations of White Privilege

- ✓ the ability to move through one's professional and personal world without any thought of race. On the other hand, skin color creates challenges for Black people. (**Everyone** has challenges in life, for White people it just means that their skin color is not one of the things that makes life challenging.)
- ✓ high representation in magazines, television, movies, of which blacks are often unrepresented
- ✓ positive portrayal in media vs. negative portrayal of Black people
- ✓ the presumption of innocence in any situation until proven guilty versus Black people who are usually presumed guilty until proven innocent
- ✓ believed more than Black people

  - Ex. woman in New York falsely accused a Black man of attacking her because she was offended that he asked her to put her dog on a leash. The video proved that it was not true. However, in those cases, if there is no video, the White person's word is automatically believed

- ✓ not being considered "suspicious" when doing regular behaviors
  - shopping in a store without being followed or questioned
  - being able to house hunt in an affluent neighborhood without having the police being called
- ✓ the privilege of moving into an area and neighbors will be neutral and pleasant
- ✓ assumption of earned achievements versus assuming Black people did not earn their accomplishments

If you are a White person, how do you react to the term White privilege? Do you recognize the advantage based upon the limited examples above?

_____

_____

_____

Can you think of more examples of White privilege?

_____

_____

_____

If you are a Black person, what impact has White privilege had in your life?

_____

_____

_____

IN CLOSING

- Conversations on racism are difficult, but they are necessary for racial reconciliation, especially in the Church.
- Overcoming the hurdles and roadblocks of **blind spots**, a **lack of empathy**, and **denial** are essential to having productive conversations. Purposely ensuring you increase your awareness (through prayer, unbiased feedback, and conversations) is a good first step.

SELF-REFLECTION

Overcoming blind spots, denial, and a lack of empathy is important for racial reconciliation. Pray about today's lesson and ask God to help you.

It is hard to change what you cannot see. How can you increase your awareness of your blind spots?

As it relates to empathy, how empathetic are you? Respond to the following statements to assess yourself.

I feel sad when the people around me feel sad.	Agree / Disagree / Neutral
It upsets me to see Black people being treated disrespectfully.	Agree / Disagree / Neutral
I find it hard to see why people get upset about racial issues.	Agree / Disagree / Neutral
It is difficult to see things from the other person's point of view.	Agree / Disagree / Neutral
I give equal attention to people regardless of race.	Agree / Disagree / Neutral

How did you do? Name at least 3 adjustments you can make. How will you make them?

_____

_____

_____

_____

_____

_____

ONE ACTION

What is one thing that you can do that will help you to step outside of your comfort zone and practice what you've learned?

Example(s):

- *Have an open, honest conversation with someone of a different race to talk about their experiences (may need to have some guidelines and boundaries set up) or host a small group.*
- *Volunteer at an organization that works with people of a different culture and social-economic levels to see and hear their stories.*
- *Research "redlining discrimination" to help you gain knowledge. Doing this type of research will help you begin to overcome the roadblocks of denial (systemic racism / White privilege) and the lack of empathy.*

SESSION 7 – LESSONS FROM A CHRISTIAN RACIST

Can a person be a Christian and be racist? Explain your answer.

_____

_____

_____

THE ROOTS OF RACISM

The root system of a plant provides water and food to the plant from the soil and keeps the plant upright (in place), preventing it from falling over. **There are also roots that feed, maintain, and keep racism in place.**

According to the Bible, the Apostle Peter was a Christian racist. By referencing him as a character study, we see the roots of racism manifested. The four roots are (1) *pride*, (2) *superiority*, (3) *ignorance*, and (4) *fear*.

ROOT 1: PRIDE

God gave Peter a vision. In the vision, there was a sheet of animals (clean and unclean).

We see that God was saying one thing ("Rise, Peter; kill and eat"), but Peter was saying another thing ("Not so.").

This happened three times.

This is **pride**.

ACTS 10:13-16 (KJV)

[13] And there came a voice to him, Rise, Peter; kill, and eat. [14] But Peter said, Not so, Lord; for I have never eaten any thing that is common or unclean. [15] And the voice *spake* unto him again the second time, What God hath cleansed, *that* call not thou common. [16] This was done thrice: and the vessel was received up again into heaven.

88

Pride says, "I think, and I feel."

Pride keeps people from acknowledging their shortcomings, weaknesses, and/or sins.

Pride keeps people from repenting and accepting responsibility without justification or excuses.

Pride talks when one should be listening.

POWER POINT:

Never allow pride to keep you from acknowledging a shortcoming, weakness, or sin. Racism is sin.

Can you give examples of how pride influences racism on the job, in church, in relationships, and/or everyday life?

_____

_____

_____

Has God ever said one thing to you, and you said another? Please explain.

_____

_____

_____

- *Did you know it was prideful?*

_____

_____

Are you a prideful person? Consider the following questions:

- *Do you find yourself interrupting people when they are talking?*

  _____

- *Do you find yourself looking down on others who are of another race?*

  _____

- *Do you find yourself thinking less of others who are not as educated, affluent, or successful as yourself?*

  _____

- *Do you find it difficult to admit when you have done something wrong?*

  _____

- *Do you become defensive when you are criticized or corrected?*

  _____

If you answered "yes" to any of these questions, would you consider PRIDE as the underlying factor? If not, what do you consider this negative behavior?

_____

_____

_____

_____

- *What can you do to begin to overcome pride?*

  _____

  _____

  _____

ROOT 2: SUPERIORITY (SUPERIORITY COMPLEX)

The Holy Spirit instructed Peter to cross over racial lines and to go to Cornelius' house and share the Word of God. Peter was a Jew; Cornelius was a Gentile. Notice Peter's greeting in Acts 10:28 (NLT), "Peter told them, "You know it is against our laws for a Jewish man to enter a Gentile home like this or to associate with you. But God has shown me that **I should no longer think of anyone as impure or unclean.**" Peter believed he was superior to the Gentiles because of his racial and religious heritage.

A feeling of superiority hinders fellowship and mutual respect. It is impossible to simultaneously look down on people and operate on a level of equality. And you cannot always be looking up at someone else and feel equal to others. **Equality says that we look at each other.**

POWER POINT: **It requires biblical mind renewal and intentionality for some White people (White Christians) to not feel SUPERIOR to Black people.**	
White people are the majority race in America. The White American population is around 64%.	Black people are the minority race in America. The Black American population is around 12%-13%.
There is a huge wealth, position, and authority gap between Whites and Blacks.	
White people usually operate on the "giving" side. Generally, White people give to and help Black people.	Black people usually operate on the "receiving" side. Generally, Black people receive from White people.
White people do not usually feel a need for "Black contributions" (except maybe in athletics).	Black people usually feel a need for "White contributions."
POWER POINT: **It requires biblical mind renewal and intentionality for some Black people to not feel INFERIOR to White people.**	

How can an attitude of superiority and/or inferiority damage relationships with others (in church, family, etc.)?

_____

_____

_____

How can embracing an attitude of equality overcome racism and build effective relationships between races?

_____

_____

_____

Describe how one would go from an attitude of superiority/inferiority to a mindset of equality?

_____

_____

_____

ROOT 3: IGNORANCE

In Acts 10:28 (NLT), Peter said, "**But God has shown me** that I should no longer think of anyone as impure or unclean."

- **Ignorance** can be the absence of knowledge.
  Peter acknowledged his ignorance, in his response. God gave Peter more insight and knowledge. Peter didn't know that the wall dividing the Jew and the Gentile had been broken down through the finished work of Jesus on the Cross.
- **Ignorance** can be the embracing of false knowledge.
- **Ignorance** can lead to stereotypes and generalizations.

Dr. Martin Luther King, Jr. said that "Nothing in all the world is more dangerous than sincere ignorance..." What does this statement mean to you?

_____

_____

_____

How does ignorance reinforce racist beliefs?

_____

_____

_____

Can you admit that you do not know all there is to know about race, racism, and racial reconciliation? Why or why not?

_____

_____

_____

Share how a person can become more informed to overcome racist beliefs.

_____

_____

_____

What can churches do to help Christians and others become more informed about race, racism, and racial equality?

_____

_____

_____

ROOT 4: FEAR

In Acts 10, the Holy Spirit instructed Peter (a Jew) to cross racial lines and preach the Gospel of Jesus to the Gentiles. According to the next chapter, **"soon the news reached the apostles and other believers in Judea that the Gentiles had received the word of God. But when Peter arrived back in Jerusalem, the Jewish believers criticized him.** 'You entered the home of Gentiles and even ate with them!' they said" Acts 11:1-3 (NLT emphasis added).

Galatians 2:12 (NLT) tells us, "When he first arrived, he ate with the Gentile believers, who were not circumcised. **But afterward, when some friends of James came, Peter wouldn't eat with the Gentiles anymore. He was afraid of criticism from these people** who insisted on the necessity of circumcision."

Peter was **afraid** of the criticism.

Fears that *Christians* must overcome:

- Fear of the unknown (Different cultures, backgrounds, etc.)
- Fear of rejection (Will they accept me?)
- Fear of criticism (What will my family, friends, or peers think?)
- Fear of harm (Will I be safe?)
- Fear of loss (Will I lose support, money, church members, friends, family, position?)

Has fear influenced your **beliefs, attitudes,** *and/or* **behaviors** *on matters of race? Why or why not?*

_____

_____

_____

_____

What underlying fears have shown up in your life? Identify the fears you need to address. What can you do to overcome them? (Examples: peer pressure, rejection, harm, loneliness, failure, etc.)

_____

_____

_____

REMEDIES TO OVERCOME RACISM

The Apostle Peter was delivered from racism. Anyone can be delivered from racism.

Remedy	Definition	Remedy-in-Action in Peter's Life
Prayer	Communication (listening and speaking) with God	**Acts 10:30, 9 (NLT)** • In prayer, Cornelius had a vision in which he was instructed by an angel to send for Peter. • In prayer, Peter had a vision and was instructed by the Holy Spirit to go to Cornelius' house • It removes blind spots, creates empathy, and overcomes denial.
Epiphany	An illuminating discovery or realization; a moment of sudden or great revelation that changes you in some way	**Acts 10:28 (NLT)** • Initially, Peter didn't know that he was a racist. • Peter had a revelation of his own racist attitude and feelings of superiority.
Obedience to the Holy Spirit	Submitting to the will of God by following the directions of the Holy Spirit (from the inside, out)	**Acts 10:19 (NLT)** • The Holy Spirit led Peter to cross over and engage a different race and culture. • Oftentimes God's leadings will contradict our feelings and opinions and direct us outside of our comfort zone.

Remedy	Definition	Remedy-in-Action in Peter's Life
Acclimation	Occurs when adjusting to a new climate, a new situation, a new culture, or a new environment	• Acclimation involves initial discomfort. • **POWER POINT**: A Church in disunity has no authority to speak to a divided land. • Most multiracial local churches become diverse by minorities assimilating into predominantly White churches, not vice versa. **Acts 10:3, 5 (NLT)** • God instructed Cornelius and Gentile servants to go to where Peter was residing. God gave Peter a vision, and Peter went to Cornelius' home. God was working on both sides.
Confrontation	To come face to face with and deal with hypocrisy, differences, conflict, compromise, silence, and to hold others accountable	• You cannot change what you are not willing to confront. • Accountability is critical to overcoming racism. **Galatians 2:11 (NLT)** • When Peter out of fear acted in a racially insensitive and prejudiced way toward the Gentiles, the Apostle Paul confronted him and pointed out his hypocrisy.
Mind Renewal	The **process** of exchanging your thoughts and feelings for God's thoughts and feelings.	**Romans 12:2 (KJV)** • Mind renewal is an exchange that leads to change. • Mind renewal involves embracing "In-Christ" realities. • Mind renewal involves broadening your knowledge base (Example: learning about the roles of Black people in Bible History, World History and American History, etc.).

You are a spirit, who has a soul (mind, will, emotions), who lives in a body. When you become a Christian, they become new on the inside (spirit), but nothing happens with the mind (soul). As a result, you will have the same way of thinking (mindset) as you did before. That thinking has been shaped by authority figures, environment, repetitious information, associations, and experiences *(negative or positive)*.

Romans 12:2 says, "and do not be conformed to this world, but be transformed by the renewing of your mind, that you may prove [demonstrate, discern] what *is* that good and acceptable and perfect will of God" (NKJV emphasis added). We exchange our thoughts and our feelings for God's thoughts. **But remember, mind renewal is a process.** It will not happen overnight.

We are going to have to renew our minds to in-Christ realities about who we are, where we are, what we have, and what we can do in Christ.

If a person was brought up in a racist environment, becoming a Christian does not change that. **It takes intentionality and the renewing of the mind to break the root of racism.** We must be deliberate and consistent to be transformed by the renewing of our minds.

> **POWER POINT:**
>
> It is going to take the remedy of **mind renewal** to intentionally change the way you have viewed race.

At the beginning of this session the question was posed, "can a Christian be a racist?" Reflect on your answer. Has it changed? Why or why not?

_____

_____

_____

IN CLOSING

- Christians should not be racist. It goes against God's Word.
- By referencing the Apostle Peter as a character study, we discover roots and remedies to racism.
- White and Black people MUST undergo biblical mind renewal and be intentional in order to see themselves as equal to each other.

SELF-REFLECTION

Think about your life. Are there areas where pride, superiority, ignorance, and/or fear has been a barrier to overcoming racism?

_____

God said one thing and Peter said something different. What has kept you from doing something you know God told you to do?

_____

_____

_____

ONE ACTION

What is one thing that you can do that will help you to step outside of your comfort zone and practice what you've learned?

Example(s): *What steps can you take to renew your mind to help overcome the root of racism? What would you like to change?*

- *Meditate on Scriptures*
- *Pray*
- *Read books*
- *Watch videos*
- *Have honest conversations on racism with other races*
- *Ask a scholar who knows about the subject matter*
- *Poll people on social media*
- *Take a course*

ABOUT MIKE MOORE

Mike Moore is the founder and president of Mike Moore Ministries and author of numerous books including the popular *"Weep Not: Overcoming Grief, Disappointment, and Loss"* and *"Moving from Tragedy to Triumph."* He built this global ministry decades ago upon the simple yet profound truth that "The Word of God is the Answer" for every situation. His easy-to-follow messages provide practical ways to apply God's Word to every day, real life circumstances.

He is the Senior Pastor of Faith Chapel. In addition to providing spiritual mentorship to an alliance of pastors, Moore can be seen on his *Answers That Work* television broadcast, YouTube channel, **How To Win** podcast, and at conferences. He is married to Kennetha and they have two adult children, Michael K. and Tiffany.

ABOUT MIKE MOORE MINISTRIES

Mike Moore Ministries was built upon the simple yet profound truth that "The Word of God is the Answer" to all of life's questions. Through various mediums which include television, digital, and print, Mike Moore teaches that God wants His people to live a prosperous life that encompasses spiritual prosperity, physical health, relationships, mental health, and financial independence.

Additional resources from Mike Moore can be obtained by visiting: **mikemooreministries.org** or by calling toll free **1-866-930-WORD (9673).**

CPSIA information can be obtained
at www.ICGtesting.com
Printed in the USA
BVHW070718201120
593719BV00012B/854

9 781733 371636